Dresden Plate Quilt

a simplified method

by Wendy Gilbert

To my husband, Pete, who has supported and encouraged me in all my sewing adventures. And my two blossoming quilters, Jody and Tony, whose enthusiasm is unbreakable. Thanks for your support!

Published by:
Quilt in a Day
1955 Diamond St.
San Marcos, Ca 92069
(619)436-8936

Printed in the United States of America

Edited by Eleanor Burns
Illustrated by Merritt Voigtlander
Photographs by Wayne Norton
Desktop Publishing by Nell Bartusch

ISBN 0-922705-17-8

Table of Contents

Introduction

I love quilts and judging from the comments of other people the Dresden Plate Quilt must be one of the most recognized and best loved quilt patterns of all time.

Its name dates back to the 1700's when the Dresden China Factory was the first in Europe to produce true porcelain. Legend has it the pattern for the Dresden Plate Quilt was created by a quilter using one of her prized Dresden Plates. She turned it upside down on a piece of paper and traced around the scalloped edges. Then she divided the scalloped circle like a pie, placed a small circle in the center, and the pattern for the Dresden Plate Quilt was born.

I started my first Dresden Plate Quilt when my daughter, Jody, was a year old. Ten years later, that quilt is still unfinished. For me, the traditional method of cutting, piecing, and hand appliqueing was extremely time-consuming and not an enjoyable project while trying to raise a toddler. Now with this simplified method, my daughter is making Dresden Plate Quilts with me and my son, Tony, is looking over her shoulder asking when he can start his quilt.

With this simplified method, the wedges are all speed cut and assembly line pieced. The completed plate is then sewn to the background square, using a new technique called The Invisible Applique Stitch. This easy technique eliminates all the time consuming hand appliqueing, yet gives the look of an antique quilt without any of the handsewing. After a little practice, I was able to complete one Dresden Plate Block in less than half an hour.

Family and friends admiring your finished quilt will never know the plates on your Dresden Plate Quilt were not stitched on by hand unless you tell them. Even then, they will have to look very closely to find the invisible stitches. You might even want to keep this "Your Little Secret."

So throw off your old methods of quilting and try something new — a beautiful, unbreakable, Dresden Plate.

Wendy Gilbert

The Dresden Plate Quilt

The Dresden Plate Quilt can be made from a delightful arrangement of scrap fabrics or a planned combination of six purchased fabrics with each fabric appearing twice on the twelve wedge plate.

If you choose to do a Scrap Dresden Plate Quilt, multiply the number of blocks x 12 to give you the total number of wedges needed for your size quilt. You may want to coordinate the scrap quilt by selecting a Center Circle fabric that can be repeated in the Lattice and 9-Patch. Refer to the Yardage and Cutting Charts for your size quilt. See page 24 for directions on cutting the scrap wedges.

If you choose to do a Planned Dresden Plate Quilt, select six fabrics for the plate that coordinate well with one another. Then, from these six fabrics, choose your two or three favorites depending on the quilt size for the Lattice, 9-Patch, and Borders.

The Fit of the Quilt

The Dresden Plate Quilt Coverlet is designed for the blocks and lattice to cover the bed top and pillows. The borders hang over the sides of the bed. Plan to use a dust ruffle to finish this look.

The Dresden Plate Quilt Bedspread is designed for one half of both outside rows of blocks to hang over on each side of the bed. The quilt covers the pillows and the borders drop to the floor. If you are making a twin, double, or queen bedspread, go up one quilt size to the next Yardage and Cutting Charts.

Check the measurements under "Approximate Finished Size" on the Cutting Chart for your size quilt and compare the measurements to your bed size.

Parts of the Quilt

Plate:
  Center Circle
  Wedge

Background Square

9-Patch Square

Lattice

First Border

Second Border

Third Border

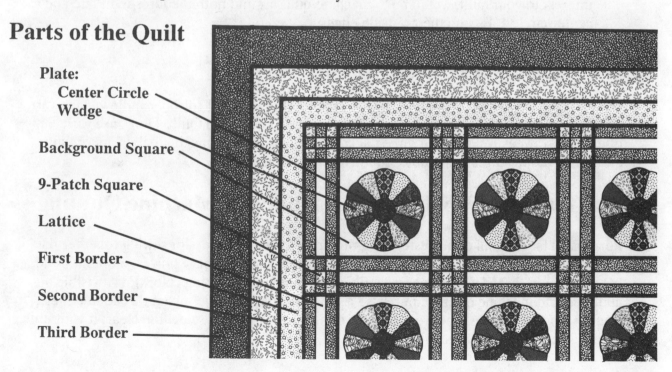

Materials and Supplies

Fabric

Select a **good quality of 100% cotton** 45" wide for your quilt top and backing. **Do not use blends!** Definitely do not mix one blend with cottons! If you wish, prewash the lights and darks separately with soap in a gentle wash cycle. If you do not prewash your fabric, carefully hand wash your quilt in cold water with a delicate soap when it becomes soiled.

Batting

Select bonded polyester batting for the inside of your quilt. Check for a brand of bonded batting that has not been treated with formaldehyde and has no "needle drag." It should feel soft to the touch and not fall apart when tugged. The thickness of the batting you choose is very important.

Thick Batting, 8 oz.-10 oz.

These battings show the most dimension when tied and are the warmest. Due to their thickness, however, they are difficult to machine quilt. Therefore, if you use thick batting, finish the Dresden Plate Quilt using the Quick Turn Method (page 54), tie or machine quilt around one or two borders, and tie the rest of the quilt.

Thin Batting, 2 oz.-3 oz.

A thin batting is best for hand or machine quilting. With this batting, finish the Dresden Plate Quilt with either the Quick Turn Method (page 54) or the Machine Quilting and Binding Method (page 58). Then machine quilt by "Stitching in the Ditch" (page 57) the outside edges of both the vertical and horizontal Lattice and 9-Patch Square and then around each border. An optional feature, which adds dimension and interest to your quilt, would be to machine quilt around both the Dresden Plate and the center circle 1/4" from their outside edges.

Thread for Tying the Quilt

Use six strands of embroidery floss, or use crochet thread, pearl cotton, candlewicking yarn, or 100% wool yarn for tying down the blocks on the Quick Turn Quilt. Don't use yarns or fibers that fray easily. Purchase three packages of floss for wallhanging/baby, lap, or twin quilts, and six packages for double, queen or king quilts.

Thread for Quilt Top, Invisible Applique, & Machine Quilting

Purchase a large spool of polyester spun thread in a neutral shade for sewing together the blocks and borders of the quilt top. Purchase another large spool of polyester spun thread, for the bobbin thread when machine quilting, to match the backing color. For invisible applique and machine quilting, purchase a spool of fine "invisible" nylon thread in either clear or smokey for the top thread. If your quilt is light in color, select the clear; if your quilt is dark in color, select the smokey.

Notions

Rotary Cutter and Gridded Mat
Use a large industrial size rotary cutter capable of cutting through several layers of fabric at one time with a plexiglas ruler on a special gridded plastic mat.

Plexiglas Rulers
Use a thick 6" x 24" plexiglas ruler for accurately measuring and cutting strips, a 6" x 12" plexiglas ruler for cutting wedges and 9-patches, and a 12 1/2" square plexiglas ruler for cutting the background and lining squares.

Pins
Use extra-long 1 3/4" sharp pins with the colored heads for pinning, a curved upholstery needle for tying, and #1 nickle plated safety pins for machine quilting.

Scissors
Use an extremely sharp pair of small scissors for clipping and trimming the seams of the plate and the center circles.

Marking Pencil
Use a sharp pencil for tracing your templates and for drawing around the wedge and circle patterns on your fabric.

Template Plastic (Optional)
Use a clear or opaque template plastic for making wedge and circle patterns.

Sewing Machine
Your sewing machine must have a Blind Hem Stitch or a Zig Zag Stitch to do the Invisible Applique Stitch needed to finish the Dresden Plate Block.

Presser Foot
Use a general purpose presser foot. The sewing machine needle should hit in the center of the foot. Use the edge of the foot as a guide for a 1/4" seam allowance.

Walking Foot (Optional)
An even feed foot, or walking foot, is a useful aid while machine quilting two layers of fabric with batting. Using the walking foot keeps the three layers moving together and helps prevent shifting and distorting.

Magnetic Seam Guide
The magnetic seam guide is a powerful magnet that will not slip or move when placed on a metal throat plate against the presser foot. Use it to sew straight, consistent seams on a regular sewing machine or serger, but **do not use it on a computerized machine.**

Bicycle Clips/Trouser Bands
Wrap bicycle clips around a tightly rolled quilt when machine quilting so the quilt can fit through the "keyhole" of the machine.

General Cutting Instructions

Use a large industrial size rotary cutter with a plexiglas ruler, and a special gridded plastic mat.

1. Make a nick on the selvage edge and tear your fabric from selvage to selvage to put the fabric on the straight of the grain.

2. Fold the fabric in fourths, matching the torn straight edge thread to thread. It is often impossible to match the selvage sides.

3. Lay your fabric on the gridded mat with most of it lying off to the right.

4. Line up the quarter inch line on the ruler with the very edge of the fabric on the left.

5. Spread the fingers of your left hand to firmly hold the ruler. With the rotary cutter in your right hand, begin cutting with the blade off the fabric on the mat. Put all your strength into the rotary cutter as you cut away from you; trim the torn, ragged edge. (Reverse this procedure if you are left-handed.)

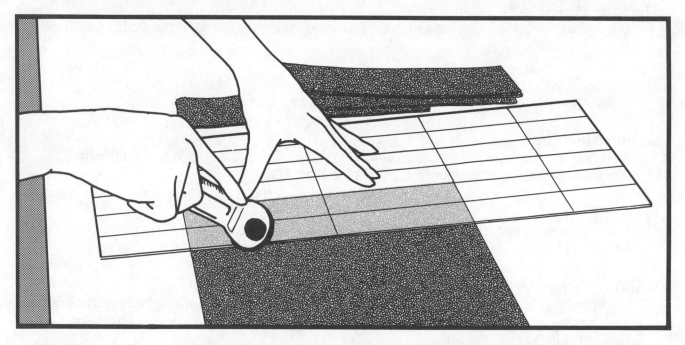

6. Use the 6" x 24" plexiglas ruler for cutting the 2" x 45" 9-patch and lattice strips.

7. Use the 12 1/2" square ruler for cutting the 11" x 45" lining strips.

8. Use the 12 1/2" square ruler for cutting the 12 1/2" x 45" background strips.

9. Follow the cutting charts for the number of strips to cut for each section of the quilt.

10. **Cut your borders only after you have completed your top and checked the fit.** All borders are cut varying widths according to the Cutting Charts.

Seam Allowance

Use an accurate and consistent 1/4" Seam Allowance!

The width of the presser foot usually determines the seam allowance. Line the edges of the fabric with the edge of the presser foot and sew a few stitches. Measure the seam allowance. If it is 1/4", **a magnetic seam guide** placed on the metal throat plate against the presser foot will assure a consistent 1/4" seam. If the measurement is less than 1/4", place the magnetic seam guide at a slight distance from the presser foot for a consistent 1/4" seam. If the seam allowance measures more than 1/4", you may be able to adjust the needle position or feed the fabric so that it doesn't come to the edge of the presser foot.

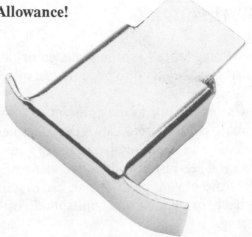

Consistency in your sewing is most important to achieve. If you are able to adjust your seam to within 1 or 2 threads of a 1/4" seam, and you are consistent, the finished quilt should match beautifully.

Use 15 Stitches Per Inch!

Set your machine at the tight stitch, 15 stitches per inch, or a #2 on machines with stitch selections from #1 - #4. This tight stitch is used because backstitching is rarely done in assembly line sewing.

Option of Using the Overlock Machine

The overlock may be used for the straight strip piecing of the 9-Patch, Lattice, and sewing the quilt pieces together. A magnetic seam guide can also be used on an overlock if a fabric guide has not been provided. A five thread overlock with a chain safety stitch is the preferred overlock for strip quilting perfect 1/4" seams. **Definitely do not trim away any part of the seam allowance with your knife as you sew.** Trim off only the "whiskers" from frayed edges.

Three Thread Overlocks

If you can only adjust your seam to 1/8" or 3/16", consider cutting your strips 1/8" or 1/16" smaller initially and all the way through! With an extra 1/8" added to every strip and block in every row, there would be a sizeable difference in the overall finished size. Adjust your knife and your 1/4" seam allowance so you don't trim away part of the seam allowance with the knife as you sew.

If you make an adjustment at this point, you must use this size throughout all steps.

Color and Fabric Selection

Fabrics 1 through 6

When selecting fabrics for the plate, colors in the medium to dark range work best. Avoid light fabrics, as they tend to become lost against the light background fabric.

Begin by selecting one fabric as an interesting large scaled print fabric that includes several of your main colors. Break down that one piece into separate colors, and select more fabrics in those colors in a progressive range of values from medium to dark. Line up the bolts of fabrics so you see just the edges and can easily find which colors go well beside each other. Vary the scale of your prints for an exciting finished look to your plate. Consider including a stripe, check, or plaid fabric. Quilts made with fabrics using the same scale of design tend to look boring.

Dresden Plate Center Circle, Fabric CC

Center Circles can be a repeat of one of your wedge fabrics, a solid color fabric, or any other coordinating fabric you like. If you choose a light fabric and the sewn wedges of the plate show through 2 layers of the Center Circle fabric, add an extra layer of lining before sewing.

Remainder of the Dresden Plate Quilt

Fabric L, or light, is the plate lining, the background square of the Dresden Plate Block, and the middle fabric of the lattice strips. This fabric must be a full 45" wide or you will need extra fabric.

Fabric M, or medium, is the predominate fabric of the 9-patch, and the first or second border depending on your quilt size. It can also be used for the backing and binding.

Fabric D, or dark, is the two outside fabrics of the lattice strip, the secondary fabric of the 9-patch, and the second or third border depending on your quilt size. It can also be used for the backing and binding.

Quilt Variations

Substitute:
∘ a lengthwise directional stripe or a floral print for the Lattice Strips

∘ a solid square for the 9-Patch Square

∘ a light-colored Dresden Plate with a dark Background Square

∘ 2, 3, or 4 coordinating fabrics instead of 6 for the Dresden Plate

Dresden Plate Paste-Up Block

Cut out small swatches of your fabrics and paste them in place with a glue stick to visualize how your finished block will look before you begin sewing. Paper backed fusing web can also be used in place of a glue stick. Follow the manufacturer's directions for fabric; it works the same on paper.

Wedge Colors

1	2	3	4	5	6

M	D	M	D				M	D	M
D	M	D	L				D	M	D
M	D	M	D				M	D	M

D	L	D	CC 1 2 3 4 5 6	D	L	D

L

M	D	M	D				M	D	M
D	M	D	L				D	M	D
M	D	M	D				M	D	M

CC-Center Circle   L-Light   M-Medium   D-Dark

Wallhanging or Baby Quilt

4 Dresden Plate Blocks

Yardage Chart

Fabric	Blocks	Lattice with 9-Patch	Borders
6 Medium or Dark Wedge Fabrics	1/4 yd. of each or scraps		
Center Circle (CC)	1/4 yd.		
Light (L) Lining, Background, and Lattice	1 1/4 yds.	1/3 yd.	
Medium (M) 9-Patch		1/4 yd.	First 3/8 yd.
Dark (D) 9-Patch & Lattice		2/3 yd.	Second 5/8 yd.
Backing			3 yds.
Binding (Optional)			2/3 yd.
Batting			52" x 52"
Approximate Finished Size:			48" Square

Cutting Chart

Fabric	Blocks	Lattice with 9-Patch	Borders
6 Medium or Dark Wedge Fabrics	8 Wedges of each fabric or 48 Wedges		
Center Circle (CC)	Cut Later		
Light (L) Lining, Background, and Lattice	(1)11" x 45" (.2)12 1/2" x 45"	(4) 2" x 45"	
Medium (M) 9-Patch		(3) 2" x 45"	First (4) 2 1/2" x 45"
Dark (D) 9-Patch & Lattice		(10) 2" x 45"	Second (5) 3 1/2" x 45"
Backing			One piece
Binding (Optional)			(5) 3 3/4" x 45"

Lap Quilt

6 Dresden Plate Blocks

Yardage Chart

Fabric	Blocks	Lattice with 9-Patch	Borders
6 Medium or Dark Wedge Fabrics	1/4 yd. of each or scraps		
Center Circle (CC)	1/4 yd.		
Light (L) Lining, Background, and Lattice	1 1/2 yds.	1/2 yd.	
Medium (M) 9-Patch		1/3 yd.	First 1/2 yd.
Dark (D) 9-Patch & Lattice		1 1/8 yds.	Second 2/3 yd.
Backing			3 yds.
Binding (Optional)			7/8 yd.
Batting			52" x 68"

Approximate Finished Size: 48" x 64"

Cutting Chart

Fabric	Blocks	Lattice with 9-Patch	Borders
6 Medium or Dark Wedge Fabrics	12 Wedges of each fabric or 72 Wedges		
Center Circle (CC)	Cut Later		
Light (L) Lining, Background, and Lattice	(2)11" x 45" (2)12 1/2" x 45"	(6) 2" x 45"	
Medium (M) 9-Patch		(4) 2" x 45"	First (5) 2 1/2" x 45"
Dark (D) 9-Patch & Lattice		(16) 2" x 45"	Second (5) 3 1/2" x 45"
Backing			2 equal pieces
Binding (Optional)			(6) 3 3/4" x 45"

Twin Quilt

10 Dresden Plate Blocks

Yardage Chart

Fabric	Blocks	Lattice with 9-Patch	Borders Coverlet	Borders Bedspread
6 Medium or Dark Wedge Fabrics	1/3 yd. of each or scraps		First 3/4 yd.	Buy
Center Circle (CC)	1/4 yd.			Fabric
Light (L) Lining, Background, and Lattice	2 1/2 yds.	3/4 yd.		& Sew
Medium (M) 9-Patch		1/2 yd.	Second 1 1/3 yds.	According
Dark (D) 9-Patch & Lattice		1 1/3 yds.	Third 2 yds.	to Double
Backing			6 3/4 yds.	Size
Binding (Optional)			1 1/8 yds.	Coverlet
Batting			69" x 118"	
Approximate Finished Size:			65" x 114"	81" x 114"

Cutting Chart

Fabric	Blocks	Lattice with 9-Patch	Borders Coverlet	Borders Bedspread
6 Medium or Dark Wedge Fabrics	20 Wedges of each fabric or 120 Wedges		First (7) 3" x 45"	Cut Fabric
Center Circle (CC)	Cut Later			&
Light (L) Lining, Background, and Lining	(3)11" x 45" (4)12 1/2" x 45"	(9) 2" x 45"		Sew According
Medium (M) 9-Patch		(5) 2" x 45"	Second (8) 5" x 45"	to
Dark (D) 9-Patch & Lattice		(22) 2" x 45"	Third (9) 7" x 45"	Double Size
Backing			2 equal pieces	Coverlet
Binding (Optional)			(9) 3 3/4" x 45"	

Double Quilt

15 Dresden Plate Blocks

Yardage Chart

Fabric	Blocks	Lattice with 9-Patch	Borders Coverlet	Borders Bedspread
6 Medium or Dark Wedge Fabrics	1/3 yd. of each or scraps		First 3/4 yd.	Buy
Center Circle (CC)	1/2 yd.			Fabric
Light (L) Lining, Background, and Lattice	3 1/4 yds.	1 yd.		& Sew
Medium (M) 9-Patch		5/8 yd.	Second 1 1/3 yds.	According
Dark (D) 9-Patch & Lattice		2 yds.	Third 2 yds.	to Queen
Backing			7 yds.	Size
Binding (Optional)			1 1/4 yds.	Coverlet
Batting			85" x 118"	
Approximate Finished Size:			81" x 114"	91" x 108"

Cutting Chart

Fabric	Blocks	Lattice with 9-Patch	Borders Coverlet	Borders Bedspread
6 Medium or Dark Wedge Fabrics	30 Wedges of each fabric or 180 Wedges		First (7) 3" x 45"	Cut Fabric
Center Circle (CC)	Cut Later			&
Light (L) Lining, Background, and Lattice	(4) 11" x 45" (5) 12 1/2" x 45"	(13) 2" x 45"		Sew According
Medium (M) 9-Patch		(7) 2" x 45"	Second (8) 5" x 45"	to Queen
Dark (D) 9-Patch & Lattice		(32) 2" x 45"	Third (9) 7" x 45"	Size
Backing			2 equal pieces	
Binding (Optional)			(10) 3 3/4" x 45"	Coverlet

Queen Quilt

20 Dresden Plate Blocks

Yardage Chart

Fabric	Blocks	Lattice with 9-Patch	Borders	
			Coverlet	Bedspread
6 Medium or Dark Wedge Fabrics	1/2 yd. of each or scraps		First 7/8 yd.	Buy
Center Circle (CC)	5/8 yd.			Fabric
Light (L) Lining, Background, and Lattice	4 1/8 yds.	1 1/2 yds.		&
Medium (M) 9-Patch		5/8 yd.	Second 1 1/4 yds.	Sew According
Dark (D) 9-Patch & Lattice		2 1/2 yds.	Third 1 5/8 yds.	to
Backing			9 1/2 yds.	King
Binding (Optional)			1 1/4 yds.	Size
Batting			95" x 112"	Coverlet
Approximate Finished Size:			91" x 108"	108" x 108"

Cutting Chart

Fabric	Blocks	Lattice with 9-Patch	Borders	
			Coverlet	Bedspread
6 Medium or Dark Wedge Fabrics	40 Wedges of each fabric or 240 Wedges		First (8) 3" x 45"	Cut
Center Circle (CC)	Cut Later			Fabric
Light (L) Lining, Background, and Lattice	(5)11" x 45" (7)12 1/2" x 45"	(17) 2" x 45"		& Sew
Medium (M) 9-Patch		(8) 2" x 45"	Second (9) 4" x 45"	According
Dark (D) 9-Patch & Lattice		(41) 2" x 45"	Third (10) 5" x 45"	to King
Backing			3 equal pieces	Size
Binding (Optional)			(10) 3 3/4" x 45"	Coverlet

King Quilt

25 Dresden Plate Blocks

Yardage Chart

Fabric	Blocks	Lattice with 9-Patch	Borders	
			Coverlet	Bedspread
6 Medium or Dark Wedge Fabrics	5/8 yd. of each or scraps		First 1 yd.	First 1 yd.
Center Circle (CC)	1 yd.			
Light (L) Lining, Background and Lattice	5 1/2 yds.	1 1/3 yds.		
Medium (M) 9-Patch		3/4 yd.	Second 1 1/3 yds.	Second 1 5/8 yds.
Dark (D) 9-Patch & Lattice		3 yds.	Third 1 5/8 yds.	Third 2 1/4 yds.
Backing			9 1/2 yds.	10 yds.
Binding (Optional)			1 1/3 yd.	1 1/2 yds.
Batting			112" x 112"	118" x 118"
Approximate Finished Size:			108" x 108"	114" x 114"

Cutting Chart

Fabric	Blocks	Lattice with 9-Patch	Borders	
			Coverlet	Bedspread
6 Medium or Dark Wedge Fabrics	50 Wedges of each fabric or 300 Wedges		First (9) 3" x 45"	First (9) 3" x 45"
Center Circle (CC)	Cut Later			
Light (L) Lining, Background, and Lattice	(7)11" x 45" (9)12 1/2" x 45"	(20) 2" x 45"		
Medium (M) 9-Patch		(10) 2" x 45"	Second (10) 4" x 45"	Second (10) 5" x 45"
Dark (D) 9-Patch & Lattice		(48) 2" x 45"	Third (10) 5" x 45"	Third (10) 7" x 45"
Backing			3 equal pieces	3 equal pieces
Binding (Optional)			(11) 3 3/4" x 45"	(12) 3 3/4" x 45"

Making the Dresden Plate Blocks

Making the Template

A template is a durable pattern that can be used over and over again. Cardboard and template plastic are both excellent for this purpose. Select one method below and make your wedge and circle templates using the patterns at the back of this book.

Method 1

Trace or copy the paper patterns on page 62. Cut out the pattern pieces leaving a small margin of paper around them. Apply paper backed fusing web or use glue stick to adhere the paper to cardboard. Old cereal boxes work well. Then cut out your pattern pieces, **very accurately**, along the solid dark lines.

Method 2

Lay clear or opaque template plastic over the paper patterns. Trace the patterns, **very accurately**, using a ruler and pencil for the wedge, and a compass for the circle. Cut out your pattern pieces, **very accurately**, along the pencil lines.

(Variation) Making One Scrap Dresden Plate Block

On the **wrong side** of two scrap fabrics draw around the wedge template using a sharp pencil.

Refer to the illustration for step #3 on the next page and layer five more scrap fabrics beneath **each** scrap fabric with a drawn wedge.

Then skip to step #2 on page 26 and continue following the directions for cutting and sewing the wedges.

Marking the Wedges for the Dresden Plate Quilt

It is important to complete the Paste-Up Block and number your wedge fabrics accordingly before drawing the wedges.

Any wedges to be cut on the diagonal will need to be drawn and cut separately.

Before drawing the wedges, refer to Step #2 and the illustration on the next page.

You should get 20 wedges across the 45" width of your fabric. If you are drawing more than one row of wedges (20 wedges), leave at least 1" between rows.

Do Not Fold Fabric.

1. Press wedge fabrics.

2. Place your template on the wrong side of wedge fabric #2 and close to the selvage edge; use a sharp pencil to draw the number of wedges needed for your size quilt. To avoid waste as you draw each wedge, turn the template so the wedges butt against each other.

Number of Wedges to Draw:
◦ Wallhanging/Baby 8
◦ Lap 12
◦ Twin 20
◦ Double 30
◦ Queen 40
◦ King 50

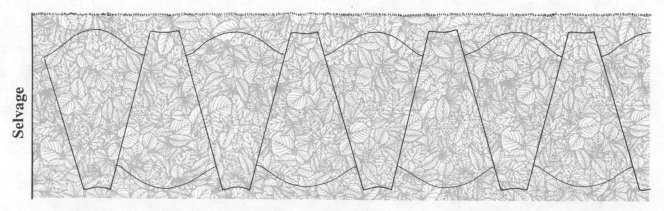

3. Stack the six wedge fabrics in the following order with fabric #5 on the bottom and fabric #2 on the top. Match the torn edges. Selvages may not match.

Lay wedge fabric #5 right side up on the cutting mat.
Lay wedge fabric #6 right side down on top of fabric #5.
Lay wedge fabric #3 right side up on top of fabric #6.
Lay wedge fabric #4 right side down on top of fabric #3.
Lay wedge fabric #1 right side up on top of fabric #4.
Lay wedge fabric #2 right side down on top of fabric #1.

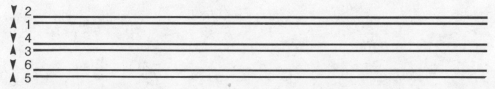

4. The wedges you drew on the wrong side of fabric #2 will now be showing on the top of the stack.
5. Check to make sure fabric #5 and #6 are right sides together, fabric #3 and #4 are right sides together, and fabric #1 and 2 are right sides together.

6. Check to make sure any narrow fabrics are fully under the end wedges.

7. Press all six layers together. This helps the fabrics stick together while cutting and sewing.

Cutting the Wedges for the Dresden Plate Quilt

1. For double, queen, or king size quilt, make a lengthwise cut through all six layers along the bottom of each row of wedges with a 6" x 24" ruler and rotary cutter. This will separate each row of wedges.

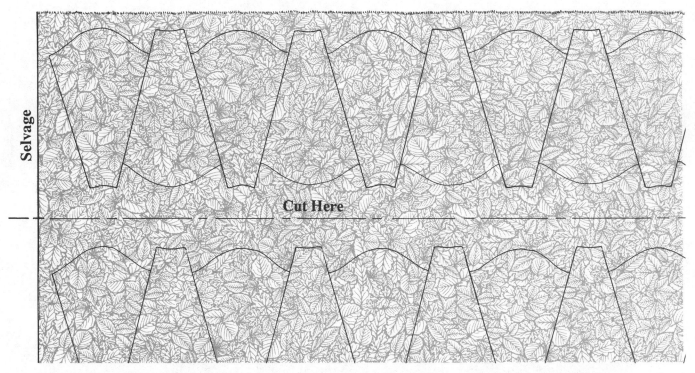

2. Cut through all six layers along the straight edge of each wedge with a 6" x 12" ruler and rotary cutter. The 6" x 12" ruler is easier to maneuver when flipping back and forth.

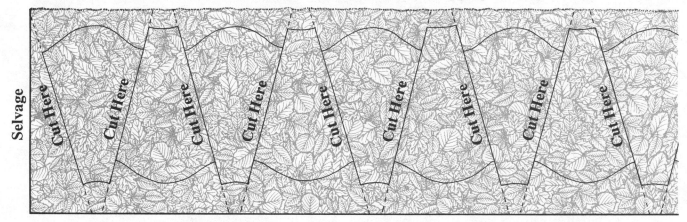

3. Place the wedge template on top of a pile of wedges. Hold the wedge template firmly with your hand or stabilize it in place with a plexiglas ruler. You may want to trim the wedges free hand without using the template or ruler. It's faster.

4. **Very carefully** trim the top and bottom curved edges of the wedges with your rotary cutter.

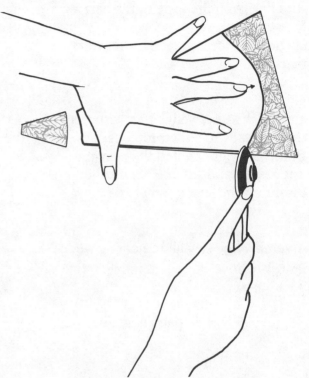

5. Repeat with each pile.

Sewing the Wedges into Pairs

1. Leave the wedges right sides together. Stack the small piles of wedges, as they were cut, into one or two large piles with the wide part of the wedges at the top.

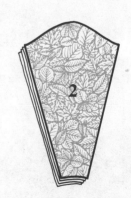

2. Place a magnetic seam guide on the throat plate of your sewing machine 1/4" away from the needle. (Not recommended for computerized machines.)
   ◦ **1/4" seam allowances**
   ◦ **15 stitches per inch**
   ◦ **Stitch accurately**
   ◦ **Do not press**
   ◦ **Do not back stitch**

3. Pick up the first wedge pair with right sides already together and top edges even.

4. Sew the first wedge pair together, stitching from the wide to the narrow.

5. Do not clip threads or remove from machine.

6. Pick up the next wedge pair with right sides already together, top edges even. Butt them right behind the previous wedge pair and stitch. This is called assembly line sewing.

7. Assembly line sew all remaining wedge pairs together.

8. Remove all wedge pairs from machine.

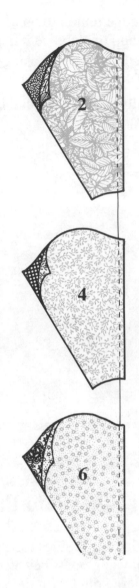

Sewing the Pairs into Plates

1. Clip the threads between pairs and stack them right side up into three piles as shown.

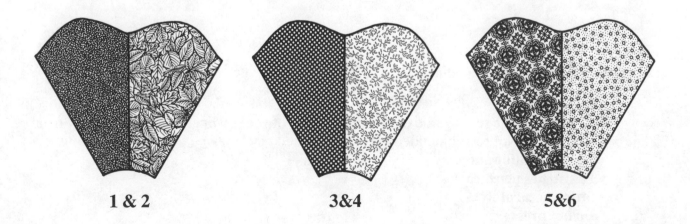

1 & 2 **3&4** **5&6**

2. Flip pair #3/4 onto pair #1/2, right sides together. Match the top edges of wedge #2 and wedge #3.

3. Stitch from the wide to the narrow.

4. Assembly line sew all pairs #1/2 and #3/4 together.

5. Clip threads between each section.

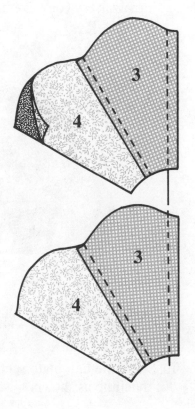

6. Restack the sewn pairs, right sides up, into two piles as shown.

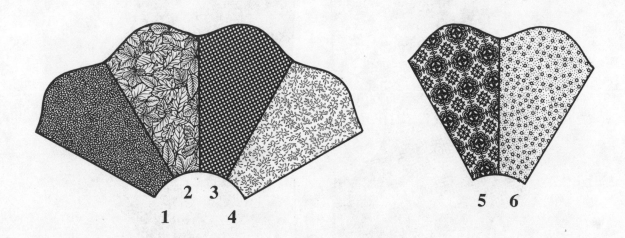

7. Flip pair #5/6 onto the already assembled 4 wedge section, right sides together. Match the top edges of wedge #4 and wedge #5.

8. Assembly line sew all remaining pairs #5/6 to 4 wedge sections. Stitch from wide to narrow. Now you have half plates.

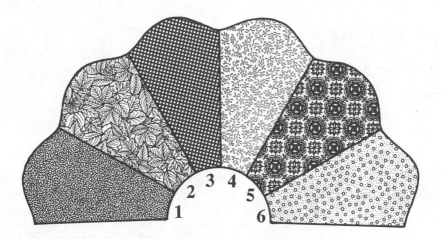

9. Clip threads between half plates.

10. Stack the half plate sections, right side up, in two equal piles next to your sewing machine as shown.

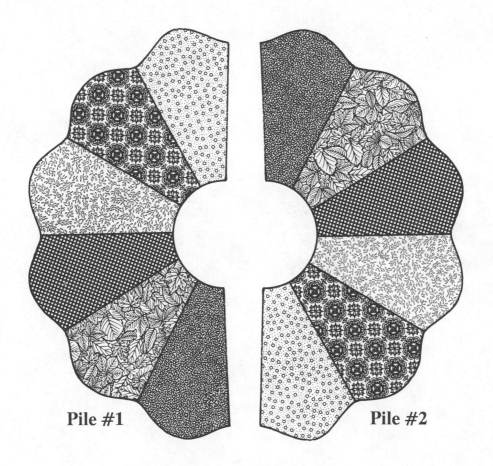

Pile #1   **Pile #2**

11. Flip a half plate section from pile #2 onto a half plate section from pile #1, right sides together. Match the outside edges of wedge #1 and #6.

12. Sew from outside edge to center, do not lift presser foot. Match the other outside edges, pull the plate slightly forward and continue sewing from center to outside edge.

13. Assembly line sew all remaining half plate sections.

14. Clip thread at center.

15. Now you have whole plates.

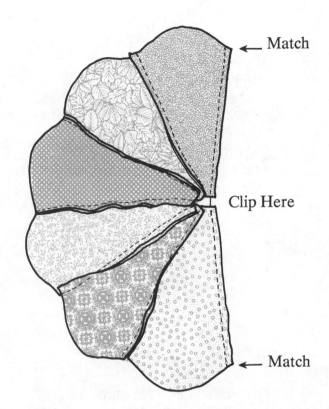

Match

Clip Here

Match

Pressing the Plate

1. Lay the plate flat on the ironing board with the wrong side up. **Press the seams in a clockwise direction.** Do not stretch out the plate.

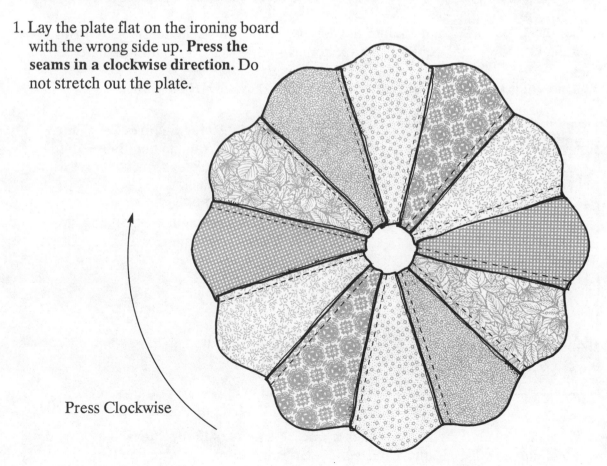

Press Clockwise

2. Turn plate to the right side and press again. **If plate does not lie flat, press from the outside edge to the center with the side of your iron.** Push any excess fabric to the center opening where it will overlap and make a small tuck. Any small tucks will be covered by the Center Circle.

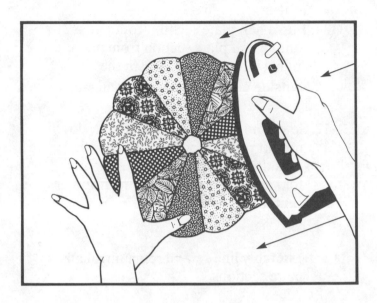

PLATE MUST LIE FLAT
AT THIS POINT!

Lining The Plate

If you have not cut the strips for the lining squares, refer to the Cutting Chart for the number of 11" x 45" lining strips needed for your size quilt. For information on cutting the 11" x 45" lining strips refer to the General Cutting Instructions on page 8.

1. Cut the 11" x 45" lining strips into the number of 11" lining squares needed for your size quilt. Use the 12 1/2" square ruler and remove selvages before cutting squares.

You should get four 11" Lining Squares from one 11" x 45" strip of fabric.

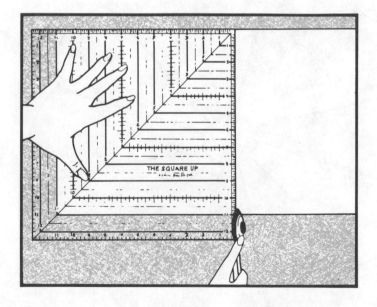

Lining Squares Per Quilt:
- Wallhanging/Baby . . . 4
- Lap 6
- Twin 10
- Double 15
- Queen 20
- King 25

2. Place each plate right sides together to one 11" square of lining. Pin well around the outer curved edges. Remove magnetic seam guide from your machine.

3. Using 15-20 stitches per inch, stitch a 1/4"
   seam around the outside edges. When you
   come to each stitching line where wedges
   were sewn, place your needle in the fabric
   on the stitching line, lift the presser foot,
   pivot your plate, put the presser foot back
   down, and continue sewing until you've
   sewn completely around the plate. Stitch
   evenly rounded edges.

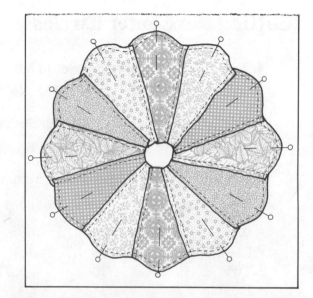

4. Trim away the seam to **1/16"**.
   (Yes, that's really 1/16".)

5. Clip at the seams being **careful** not
   to cut stitching.

6. Turn right side out through the
   center opening.

7. Work edges gently until they are
   rounded by wetting the ends of your
   fingers and rolling the seam out or use
   the eraser end of a pencil and gently
   push the seam out. Finger press each
   rounded edge.

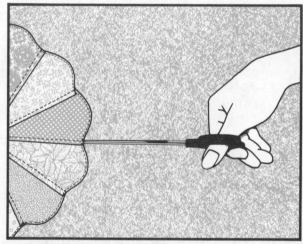

**If edges are pointed instead of rounded,
seams have probably not been trimmed
to 1/16"**

8. Turn the plate to the lining side and
   with the fingers on your left hand,
   gently pull the lining toward the center
   and away from the rounded edges while
   you are pressing the rounded edges
   with your right hand. (Reverse for
   lefties.)

9. When you are finished pressing, you
   should have evenly rounded edges and
   your lining should not show on the right
   side.

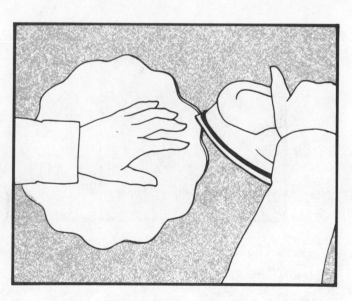

Cutting the Center Circles

1. Fold fabric for Center Circles in half **lengthwise** with right sides together. (One side will be the lining for the other side.)

2. Trace the number of Center Circles needed per quilt. Leave approximately a 1/2" margin of fabric around each circle.

You should get 10 Center Circles across the 45" width.

Center Circles Per Quilt:
- Wallhanging/Baby 4
- Lap 6
- Twin 10
- Double 15
- Queen 20
- King 25

Check to made sure the sewn wedges of the plate do not show through the two layers of Center Circle fabric. If the wedges show through, add an extra layer of lining before sewing.

3. Pin together the two layers of circle fabric. Cut apart the two layers of circles leaving the 1/2" margin.

Sewing the Center Circles

1. Match the color of thread to the color of the fabric and stitch on the traced line.

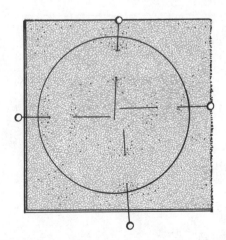

2. Trim each circle to **1/16"** from stitching line.

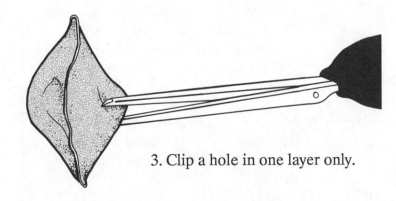

3. Clip a hole in one layer only.

4. Turn the Center Circle right side out through the hole.

5. Work edges gently until they are rounded.

If edges have points instead of rounded edges, you probably have not trimmed your seam to 1/16".

6. Press Center Circle.

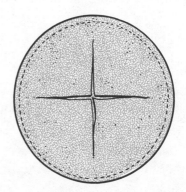

Centering the Dresden Plate on the Background Square

If you have not cut the strips for the Background Squares, refer to the Cutting Chart for the number of 12 1/2" x 45" background strips needed for your size quilt. For information on cutting the 12 1/2" x 45" background strips refer to the General Cutting Instructions on page 8.

1. Cut the 12 1/2" x 45" background strips into the number of 12 1/2" Background Squares needed for your size quilt. Use the 12 1/2" square ruler and remove selvages before cutting squares.

You should get three 12 1/2" Background Squares from one 12 1/2" x 45" strip of fabric.

Background Squares Per Quilt:
◦ Wallhanging/Baby . . . 4
◦ Lap 6
◦ Twin 10
◦ Double 15
◦ Queen 20
◦ King 25

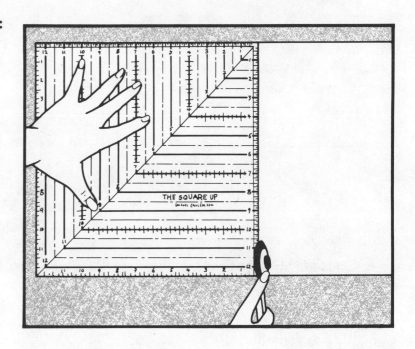

2. To find the center of the Background Square, fold the square in half making a rectangle. Press fold. Fold in half again. Press second fold.

3. To find the center of the Dresden Plate Wedges, fold the plate in half and in half again. Finger press the center of the plate lining.

4. Center the plate on the Background Square by placing a pin in the center of the plate lining and matching the pin to the center fold of the Background Square.

5. With the pin holding the centers together, spin the plate around until you like the placement of the plate on the Background Square.

There is no set way your plates must be arranged. Plates can all be arranged exactly alike or randomly.

6. Consider whether you want the center of the wedges lined up with the fold lines of the Background Square or if you prefer the seam lines of the wedge lined up with the fold lines.

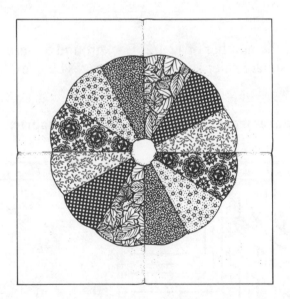 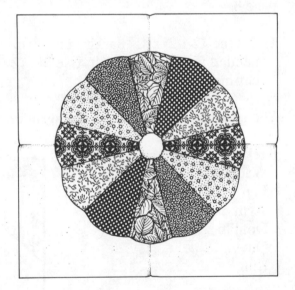

7. Pin at each wedge.

8. Center the Center Circle on the plate. Pin well to avoid tucks while sewing around the curved edges.

9. **Stop!** Lay out your Dresden Plate Blocks. Check to make sure the plates are all arranged the way you want.

Invisible Applique Technique

Sewing Dresden Plate & Center Circle to Background Square

1. Check your needle to make sure it is sharp. Use a #70 or #10.

2. Set the Blind Hem Stitch on your machine. If your machine doesn't have a Blind Hem Stitch, or if the Blind Hem Stitch catches to the right instead of to the left, you will want to use a regular zig zag stitch.

Use Zig Zag   Correct Blind
Stitch   Hem

3. Set your stitch width to approximately 1 1/2. The stitch width will vary for different machines.

4. Set your stitch length to approximately 2 for European machines or 15 stitches per inch for American machines.

5. Loosen the top tension and match your bobbin thread to the color of your Background Square.

6. Thread the soft invisible nylon thread on the top. (As you sew, watch that this nylon thread does not drop down and wrap around the thread post as you stitch. Feeding the thread from above with the use of a high thread stand prevents this.)

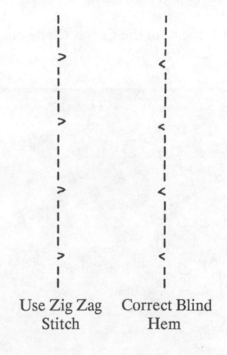

7. Sew closely around the outside edge of the plate **on the background fabric**. The Blind Hem Stitch will catch the edge of the plate.

8. Pivot at the seams.

9. Sew around the plate overlapping the stitching at the end. Set your stitch width and length to "0" and knot off the stitching. Clip threads.

10. Repeat for the Center Circle only this time stitch on the plate catching the Center Circle.

11. Repeat for each Dresden Plate and Center Circle.

12. Set blocks aside while you make the 9-Patch Squares and the Lattice Strips.

Making the 9-Patch Squares

Cut all the Lattice and 9-Patch Strips at this time. Refer to the Cutting Chart for the size quilt you are making.

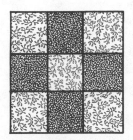

The 9-Patch Square is made up of Sections MDM and DMD.

Section MDM is used twice.
Section DMD is used once.

Making Section MDM

1. To make Section MDM, arrange your 2" x 45"strips in this order: medium, dark, medium.

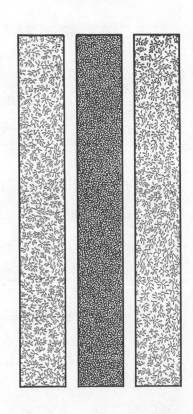

2. Stack up this many strips **in each pile** for your quilt size. (Some sizes call for half strips.)

- ◦ Wallhanging/Baby 1
- ◦ Lap 1 1/2
- ◦ Twin 2
- ◦ Double 2 1/2
- ◦ Queen 3
- ◦ King 4

3. Place the center dark strip right sides together to the first medium strip.

Use your magnetic seam guide to sew an accurate seam.

4. Stitch the length of the strip with a 1/4" seam allowance and 15 stitches per inch.

5. Do not clip threads or remove from machine.

6. Butt on and assembly line sew the next medium and dark strips until they are all stitched.

7. Open up the medium/dark strips.

8. Add the second medium strip to the
   medium/dark strip.

9. Butt on and assembly line sew as in #6.

10. Section MDM looks like this:

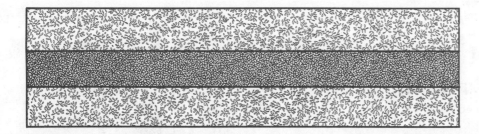

11. Carefully steam press the seams
    toward the dark strip. Press on both the
    wrong side and the right side.

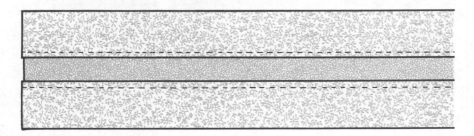

12. Layer the strips on the cutting mat. Carefully match the seams.

13. Trim the end for a right angle and to get rid of selvages. Use the rotary cutter and the
    6"x 12" ruler.

14. Cut the strips into 2" sections. You should get approximately 20 sections per strip.

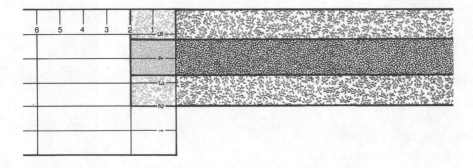

15. You need this many MDM sections for your size quilt:

- Wallhanging/Baby . . . 18
- Lap 24
- Twin 36
- Double 48
- Queen 60
- King 72

Making Section DMD

1. To make Section DMD, arrange your 2" x 45" strips in this order: dark, medium, dark.

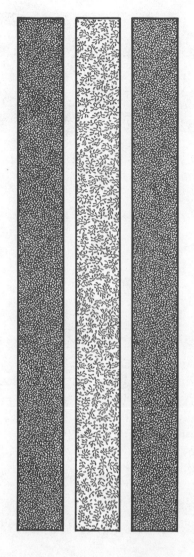

2. Stack up this many strips **in each pile** for your size quilt. (Some sizes call for half strips.)

- Wallhanging/Baby . . 1/2
- Lap 1
- Twin 1
- Double 1 1/2
- Queen 2
- King 2

3. Place the center medium strip right sides together to the first dark strip.

4. Stitch.

5. Butt on and assembly line sew the next dark and medium strips. Continue as you did when making section MDM.

6. Section DMD looks like this:

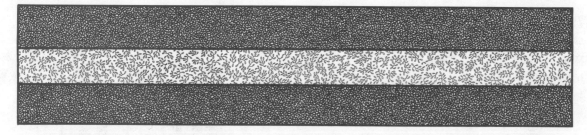

7. Carefully steam press the seams toward the dark strips. Press on both the wrong side and the right side.

8. Layer the strips on the cutting mat. Carefully match the seams.

9. Trim the end for a right angle and to get rid of selvages.

10. Cut the strips into 2" sections. You should get approximately 20 sections per strip.

11. Stack the 2" sections into one pile.

12. You need this many DMD sections for your size quilt:

- Wallhanging/Baby 9
- Lap 12
- Twin 18
- Double 24
- Queen 30
- King 36

13. Arrange the piles in MDM, DMD, MDM order.

14. Place Section DMD right sides together to Section MDM. Match the top edge.

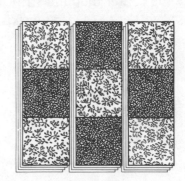

15. Stitch down about 1/2". Stretch
or ease, and fingerpin the first seam to meet.
The seam allowances go in opposite
directions and are easy to match.

16. Stitch over first seam.

17. Match and fingerpin the second seam.

18. Stitch.

19. Do not clip threads or remove from
machine.

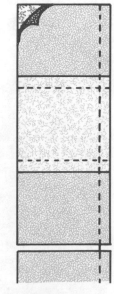

20. Butt on and assembly line sew all the first
pile of Section MDM's and Section DMD's,
matching all seams.

21. Open up MDM/DMD.

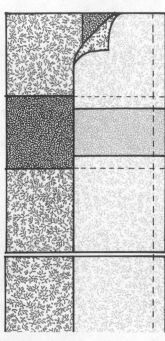

22. Assembly line sew the other Section MDM
onto the MDM/DMD's.

23. Carefully match every seam.

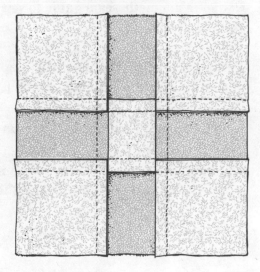

24. Clip the threads holding all the 9-Patch
Squares together.

25. Press the seams to the center.

Sewing the Lattice Strips

1. Arrange your strips in this color order: dark, light, dark.

2. Stack up this many strips **in each pile** for your size quilt:

- ° Wallhanging/Baby 4
- ° Lap 6
- ° Twin 9
- ° Double 13
- ° Queen 17
- ° King 20

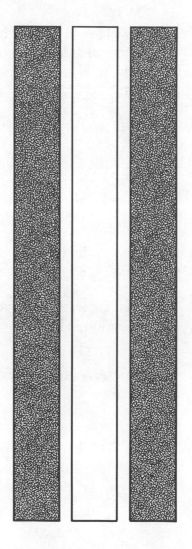

3. Place the center light strip right sides together to the first dark strip.

Use your magnetic seam guide to sew an accurate seam.

4. Stitch the length of the strip with a 1/4" seam allowance and 15 stitches per inch.

5. Do not clip threads or remove from machine.

6. Butt on and assembly line sew the next light and dark strips until they are all stitched.

7. Open up the dark/light strips.

8. Add the second dark strip to the dark/light strips.

9. Your Lattice Strips should look like this:

10. Clip the threads holding all the Lattice Strips together.

11. Carefully steam press down the middle of the light strip, pressing the seams to the dark sides. Press on both the wrong side and the right side.

12. Layer the Lattice Strips on the cutting mat. Carefully match the seams.

13. Trim the end for a right angle and to get rid of selvages. Use the rotary cutter and the 12 1/2" square up ruler.

14. Cut the Lattice Strips into 12 1/2" sections.

15. You should have this many Lattice Sections for your size quilt:

- Wallhanging/Baby . . . 12
- Lap 17
- Twin 27
- Double 38
- Queen 49
- King 60

Sewing the Quilt Top Together

Laying out the Quilt

1. Lay out the Dresden Plate Blocks, Lattice, and 9-Patch Squares by referring to the illustration opposite the Yardage and Cutting Charts for your size quilt.

2. Flip the second vertical row right sides together onto the first vertical row.

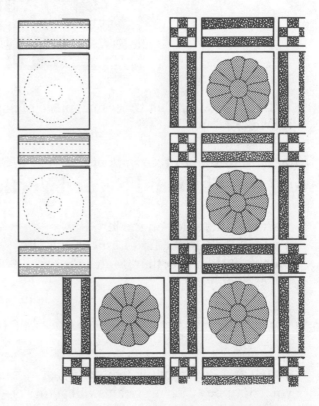

3. Start at the bottom of the first vertical row and stack up the pairs of pieces from the bottom to the top. The first pair will be on the top of your stack.

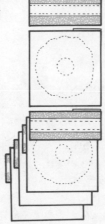

4. Stack up each one of the remaining vertical rows from the bottom to the top. The Lattice or 9-Patch at the top of the row will be on the top of the stack.

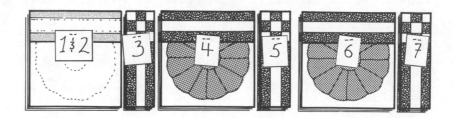

5. Write the row number on a small piece of paper and pin it through all thicknesses of fabric.

Example illustration: Your quilt may have a different number of rows.

Sewing the First and Second Vertical Rows

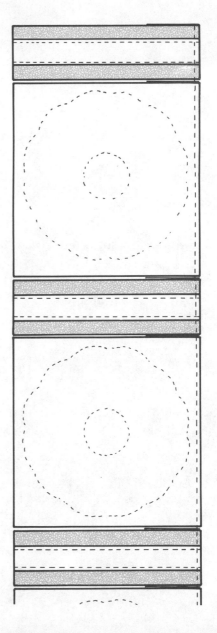

1. Start with the stack on the left, Rows 1 and 2. Pick up the first Lattice/9-Patch pair right sides together. Match the top edges evenly.

2. Backstitch and stitch down about 1/2" to anchor the two together.

3. Match and fingerpin the two seams as you continue stitching. Seams will go in opposite directions. Continue stitching making sure the bottom edges are even.

DO NOT cut threads or lift presser foot.

4. Pick up the next Dresden Plate Block/Lattice pair. Match the top edges. Butt them right behind the first pair.

5. Anchor the two pieces together. Stitch making sure the bottom edges are even. Stretch them to meet if necessary.

6. Continue going down the pile assembly line sewing the rest of the pairs.

7. Backstitch on the very last edge.

8. Remove from machine.

9. Do not cut the pairs apart.

10. Accordion fold the blocks and lattice strips starting at the bottom of the row where you have just finished sewing.

11. Lay the pile next to your sewing machine.

Sewing the Third Vertical Row

1. Place the first 9-Patch Square at the top of Row 3 right sides together to the Lattice Strip at the top of Row 2.

2. Anchor, match, fingerpin, and stitch.

3. Place the Lattice Strip of Row 3 right sides together to the Dresden Plate Block of Row 2.

4. Anchor, match, stretch to fit, and stitch.

5. Sew on all the remaining 9-Patch and Lattice Strips in Row 3 to the Lattice Strips and Dresden Plate Blocks of Row 2.

Continue to sew on all remaining rows in this manner.

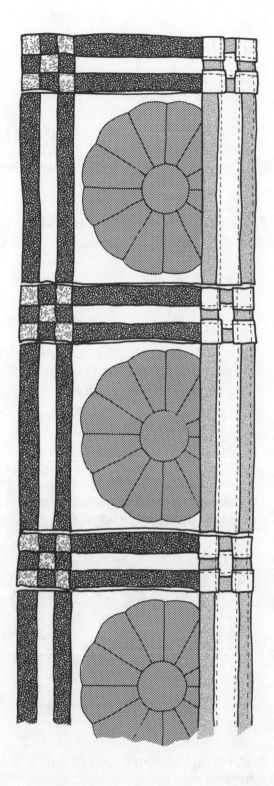

Do not clip the threads holding the Dresden Plate Blocks, Lattice and 9-Patch Squares together.

Sewing the Horizontal Rows

1. Fold the top row right sides together onto the second row.

2. Match and pin where the Blocks, Lattice, and 9-Patch Squares are joined by a thread from stitching the vertical rows.

3. The 9-Patch and Lattice seams will butt against one another and go in opposite directions. Pin if necessary.

4. The Dresden Plate Block seam allowance should be pushed away from the block and butt against the opposite seam.

5. Stretch and stitch the rows to meet.

6. Stitch all horizontal rows in the same manner.

Adding the Borders

If you wish to custom fit the quilt, lay the quilt top on your bed before you add the borders and backing. Measure to find how much border you need to get the fit you want. Keep in mind that if you use a thick batting, the quilt will "shrink" approximately 4" in length and width after completion of tying and "stitching in the ditch."

Piecing the Borders

1. Follow the Cutting Chart for the width of each border for your quilt size.

2. Cut borders across the width of the fabric from selvage to selvage. Use the rotary cutter and plexiglas ruler.

3. Square up the selvage ends, trimming off any writing.

4. Seam the strips of each border color into long pieces. Lay two strips right sides together. Match short ends. Backstitch, stitch, and backsitch again.

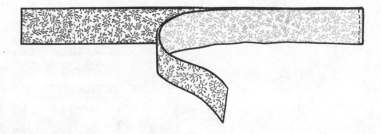

5. Take the strip on the top and fold it so the right side is up.

6. Place the third strip right side to it, backstitch, stitch, and backstitch again.

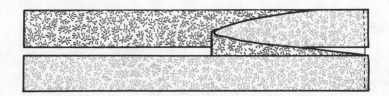

7. Continue assembly line sewing all the short ends together into one long piece.

8. Clip the threads holding the strips together.

9. Repeat for other borders.

First Border

1. Measure each long side of the quilt. Decide on an average measurement.

2. Cut two borders that measurement from the narrowest border fabric.

3. Ease and pin the borders to the long sides.

4. Stitch. Fold them out flat.

5. Press seams toward the outside edge.

6. Trim the ends of the border for a right angle. Use the 12 1/2" square ruler.

7. Measure the short sides of the quilt from one outside edge to the other, including the first long borders.

8. Cut two borders that measurement.

9. Pin the borders to the short sides.

10. Stitch. Fold them out flat.

11. Press seams toward the outside edge.

12. Trim the ends of the border for a right angle.

The ends of the borders must always be cut square to prevent "flared corners."

Repeat with any remaining border colors, working out to the widest border strips.

Finishing the Quilt

Two Different Methods for Finishing the Dresden Plate Quilt

Quick Turn Method (Pages 54 - 57)
The first method, the Quick Turn method, is the easiest and fastest method of finishing the quilt. Thick batting is "rolled" into the middle of the quilt, and the layers are held together with ties. Borders may be "stitched in the ditch" for additional dimension.

Machine Quilting and Binding Method (Pages 58 - 61)
In the second method, the three layers of backing, batting, and quilt top are machine quilted and bound with a straight grain strip of binding. A thin batting is generally used for an "old fashioned" look.

Preparing the Backing Fabric and Batting for Either Method

1. Following the Cutting Chart for your quilt, fold and cut the backing into equal pieces. If you custom fitted your quilt, you may need to adjust these measurements.

2. Tear off the selvages and seam the backing pieces together.

3. Press seams to one side.

Piecing the Bonded Batting

The batting may need to be pieced to get the desired size.

1. Cut the batting. Butt the two edges closely together without overlapping.

2. Whipstitch the edges together with a double strand of thread. Do not pull the threads tightly as this will create a hard ridge visible on the outside of the quilt.

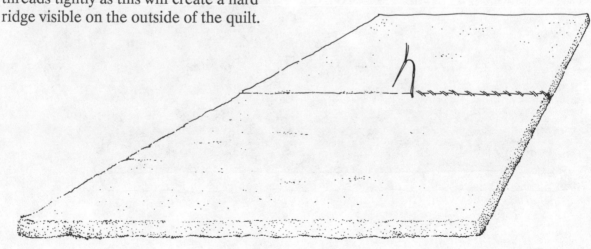

Quick Turn Method

1. Lay out the backing fabric on a large table or floor area with right side up.

2. Lay the quilt top on the backing fabric with right sides together. Stretch and smooth out the top. Pin. Trim away excess fabric. They should be the same size.

3. Stitch around the four sides of the quilt, leaving a 24" opening in the middle of one long side. Do not turn the quilt right side out.

4. Lay the quilt on top of the batting. Smooth and trim the batting to the same size as the quilt top.

5. To assure that the batting stays out to the edges, whipstitch the batting to the 1/4" seam allowance around the outside edge of the quilt.

Turning the Quilt Top

This part of making your quilt is particularly exciting. One person can turn the quilt alone, but it's fun to turn it into a 10-minute family or neighborhood event with three or four others. Read this whole section before beginning.

1. If you are working with a group, station the people at the corners of the quilt. If working alone, start in one corner opposite the opening.

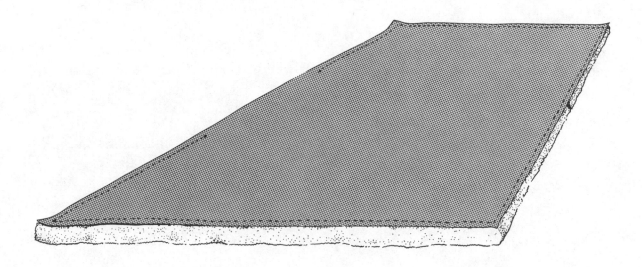

2. Roll the corners and sides tightly to keep the batting in place as you roll toward the opening.

If several people are helping, all should roll toward the opening. If only one is doing the rolling, use a knee to hold down one corner while stretching over to the other corners.

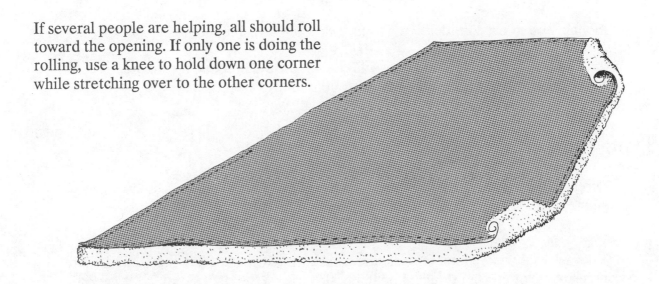

3. Open up the opening over this huge wad of fabric and batting and pop the quilt right side out through the hole.

4. Unroll carefully with the layers together.

5. Lay the quilt flat on the floor or on a very large table. Work out all wrinkles and bumps by stationing two people opposite each other around the quilt. Have each person grasp the edge and tug the quilt in opposite directions.

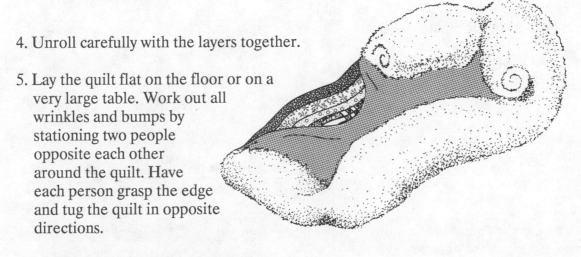

6. You can also relocate any batting by reaching inside the quilt through the opening with a yardstick. Hold the edges and shake the batting into place if necessary.

7. Slipstitch the opening shut.

Finishing the Quick Turn Quilt

You may choose to tie your entire quilt down, or machine quilt by "Stitching in the Ditch" around one or two borders and tying the rest of the quilt.

Optional: You might consider doing a bar tack using invisible thread in place of each tie.

A thick batting is difficult to machine quilt except for the borders. It is hard to get all the rolled thickness to fit through the keyhole of the sewing machine.

Tying the Quilt

1. Thread a large-eyed curved needle with six strands of embroidery floss or other thread of your choice.

If you want your square knot to show, use wool yarn. If the knot detracts from the look you want, use floss or crochet thread. For an invisible tie on the right side, pin all the points on the right side, flip the quilt to the wrong side, and tie at all pin marks.

2. Plan where you want your ties placed. A suggestion is to tie all four corners of the 9-patch square and the center circle of the Dresden Plate.

Do not tie the borders down if you wish to "stitch in the ditch."

3. Starting in the center of the quilt and working to the outside, take a 1/4" stitch through all thicknesses at the points you wish to tie. Draw the needle along to each point, going in and out, and replacing the tying material as you need it.

4. Clip all the stitches midway.

5. Tie the strands into surgeon's square knots by taking the strand on the right and wrapping it twice. Pull the knot tight. Take the strand on the left, wrap it twice, and pull the knot tight.

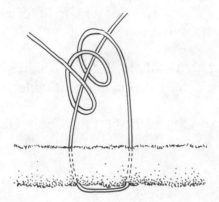 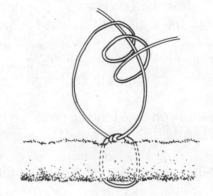

6. Clip the strands so they are 1/2" to 1" long.

Stitching in the Ditch

For more dimensional borders, you may choose to "stitch in the ditch" rather than tie the borders.

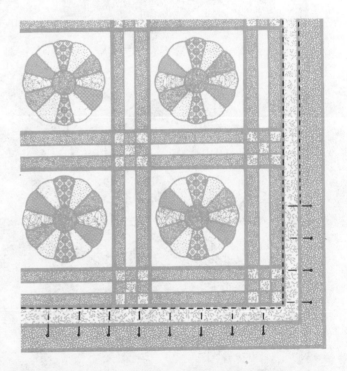

1. Change your stitch length to 10 stitches per inch. Match your bobbin color of thread to your backing color.

2. Loosen the top tension and thread the soft nylon invisible thread on the top.

3. Pin "across the ditch" the length of the borders.

4. Place the needle in the depth of the seam and stitch. Run your hand underneath to feel for puckers. If puckers occur, grasp the quilt with your left hand above the sewing machine foot, and grasp with your right hand ten inches below the sewing machine foot. Feed the quilt through the machine being careful not to stretch it as this will distort the lattice.

To avoid further puckering on the back, you may choose to use an even feed foot or walking foot, available for most sewing machines.

Machine Quilting and Binding Method

The borders and outside edges of the lattice are machine quilted using the "Stitch in the Ditch Method" described on page 57. (Optional) Dresden Plates and Center Circles can be machine quilted 1/4" from their finished edge to give them dimension.

1. Stretch out the backing right side down on a large floor area or table. Tape down on a floor area or clamp onto a table. Large binder clips are excellent as clamps for tables.

2. Place the batting on top. Lay the quilt top right side up on top of the batting. Completely smooth and stretch all layers until they are flat.

3. Pin safety pins every 5" throughout the quilt but away from the lines where you will be machine stitching.

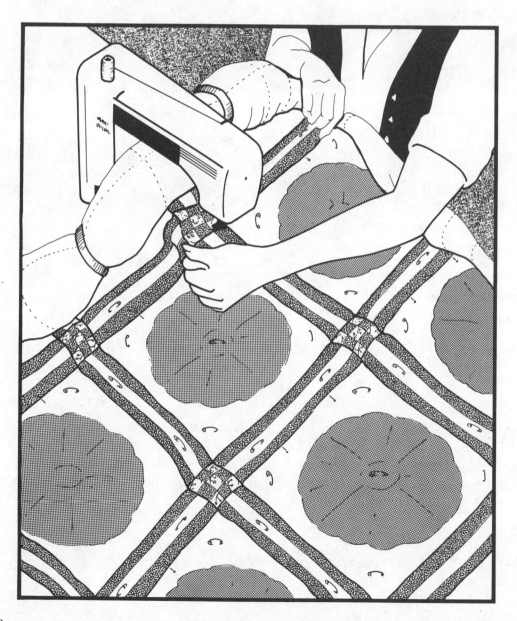

4. Trim the backing and batting to within 2" of the outside edge of the quilt.

5. Roll the quilt tightly from the outside edge in toward the middle. Hold this roll with metal bicycle clips or pins.

6. Slide this roll into the keyhole of the sewing machine.

7. Using the "Stitch in the Ditch" technique as described on page 57, sew down the long vertical outside edges of the lattice strips. Sew all the vertical seams in one direction to keep from distorting the lattice strips. Work from the center to the outside edge. Unroll and re-roll the quilt as necessary to get all the lines stitched.

8. Repeat for the horizontal sides of the lattice again sewing in only one direction to keep from distorting the lattice strips.

9. Repeat for the borders.

10. (Optional) Machine quilting around the Dresden Plates and Center Circles can be done easily on the Wallhanging/Baby or the Lap Quilt. Pin the Dresden Plate and the Center Circles through all the layers of the quilt. Sew 1/4" from the finished edge of the plate on the Background Square. Check to make sure you are not pushing the fabric and distorting your plate. Repeat for the Center Circle.

11. The larger quilts are hard to turn in a circle through the keyhole of your machine. The Dresden Plates and Center Circles of the larger quilts can be machine quilted using a free hand quilting technique. Refer to your instruction manual for directions on how to darn with your machine. You will need to use a darning foot, drop your feed dogs, and practice before attempting the free hand quilting.

Adding the Binding

1. Assembly line sew the 3 3/4" x 45" binding strips into one long strip.

Continue to use 10 stitches per inch.
Your thread should match your binding and backing. Use an even feed foot, if available.

2. Press in half lengthwise with right sides out. Turn under a 1/2" hem on the beginning narrow end of the binding strip.

3. Avoid seams hitting at corners by laying the binding around the quilt edges. Reposition if any seams are within 2" of the corner.

4. Begin applying the binding to the middle of one long side. Line up the raw edges of the binding with the raw edges of the quilt. Use **1/2" seams** and begin stitching leaving 3" of the binding to hang free.

Making the Mitered Corner

1. At the corner, stop the stitching 1/2" from the edge with the needle in the fabric. Raise the presser foot and turn the quilt to the next side. Put the foot back down.

2. Stitch backwards 1/2" to the edge, raise the presser foot, and pull the quilt forward slightly.

3. Fold the binding strip straight up on the diagonal. Fingerpress in the diagonal fold.

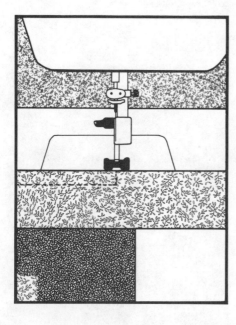

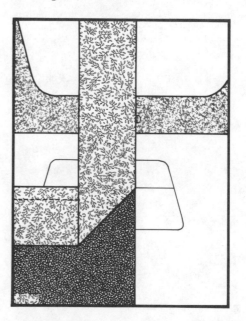

4. Fold the binding strip straight down with the diagonal fold underneath. Line up the top of the fold with the raw edge of the binding underneath.

5. Begin sewing 1/2" in from the edge at the original pivot point.

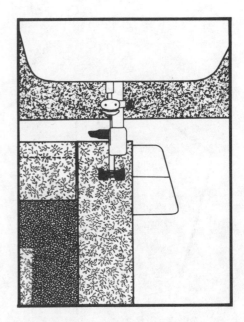

6. Continue stitching and mitering the corners around the outside of the quilt.

7. End the binding by tucking the end strip approximately 1" inside the binding strip at the beginning point.

8. Trim off any excess binding.

9. Trim the batting and backing up to the raw edges of the binding.

Turning the Binding to the Back Side of the Quilt

1. Fold the binding to the back side of the quilt.

2. Pin in place so that the folded edge on the binding covers the stitching line. Tuck in the excess fabric at the miter on the diagonal.

3. From the right side, "stitch in the ditch" around the binding. Use invisible thread on the right side of the quilt, and a bobbin thread to match the binding on the wrong side of the quilt. Catch the folded edge of the binding on the backside with the stitching.

Pattern

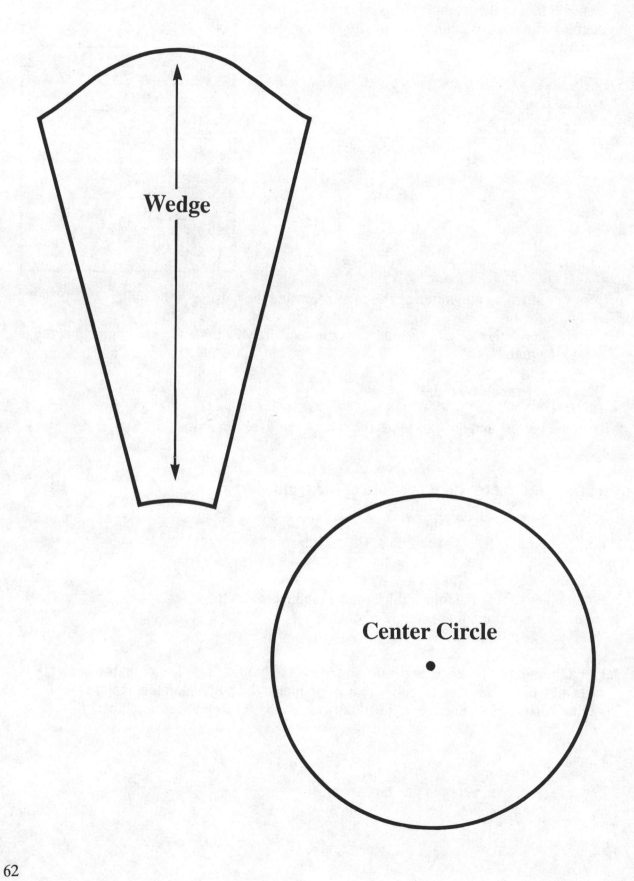

Wedge

Center Circle

Index

Acknowledgements

A heartfelt thank you to **all my students and friends** who made the first Dresden Plate Quilts! I couldn't have done it without you!

Front Cover: Lap Quilt by **Wendy Gilbert**. Sincere thanks to **Julie Gillett** and **Missy Post** who each loaned us their Grandmothers' antique china for this photograph.

Back Cover: Queen Quilt by **Wendy Gilbert**.

A special thank you to **Lee Codington** for the use of her beautiful home and assistance in setting up all the photographs.

Appreciation to **Gloria Pearce, Barbara Bredeweg,** and **Loretta Smith** for their assistance in developing and proofing the first drafts.

My gratitude to my editor, publisher, and friend, **Eleanor Burns,** for giving me the opportunity to write this book.

Order Information

If you do not have a fine quilt shop in your area, you may write for a complete catalogue of all books and patterns published by **Quilt in a Day** plus a current price list.

Books, Booklets, and Patterns by Eleanor Burns

Quilt in a Day
Log Cabin Christmas Tree Wallhanging
Diamond Vest and Strip Vest
The Sampler, A Machine Sewn Quilt
An Amish Quilt in a Day
May Basket
A Friendship Quilt
Country Christmas Sewing
Schoolhouse Wallhanging
Diamond Log Cabin Tablecloth and Treeskirt
Trio of Treasured Quilts (Monkey Wrench, Ohio Star and Bear's Paw Patterns)

Trio of Treasured Quilts
Easy Radiant Star
Dresden Plate Place Mats and Tea Cozy
Lover's Knot
Irish Chain in a Day
Morning Star Quilt
Trip Around the World Quilt
Bunnies and Blossoms
Country Patchwork Dress

Quilt in a Day
1955 Diamond Street, Unit A
San Marcos, CA 92069
Order Line: 1-800-24-KWILT (1-800-245-9458)
CA Orders and Information: 1-(619)-471-7019

If you are ever in San Diego County, southern California, drop by the Quilt in a Day Center quilt shop and classroom in the La Costa Meadows Business Park. Write ahead for a current class schedule and map.